GUIDANCE NOTE ON STATE-OWNED ENTERPRISE REFORM IN SOVEREIGN PROJECTS AND PROGRAMS

DECEMBER 2020

IAN DEVELOPMENT BANK

© 2020 Asian Development Bank
6 ADB Avenue, Mandaluyong City, 1550 Metro Manila, Philippines
Tel +63 2 8632 4444; Fax +63 2 8636 2444
www.adb.org

Some rights reserved. Published in 2020.

ISBN 978-92-9262-118-6 (print), 978-92-9262-119-3 (electronic), 978-92-9262-120-9 (ebook)
Publication Stock No. TIM210070
DOI: http://dx.doi.org/10.22617/TIM210070

The views expressed in this publication are those of the authors and do not necessarily reflect the views and policies of the Asian Development Bank (ADB) or its Board of Governors or the governments they represent.

ADB does not guarantee the accuracy of the data included in this publication and accepts no responsibility for any consequence of their use. The mention of specific companies or products of manufacturers does not imply that they are endorsed or recommended by ADB in preference to others of a similar nature that are not mentioned.

By making any designation of or reference to a particular territory or geographic area, or by using the term "country" in this document, ADB does not intend to make any judgments as to the legal or other status of any territory or area.

Corrigenda to ADB publications may be found at http://www.adb.org/publications/corrigenda.

Note:
In this publication, "$" refers to United States dollars.

On the cover: The Asian Development Bank is committed to supporting and collaborating with governments of developing member countries for planning, preparations, and implementation of state-owned enterprise reform under Strategy 2030's Operational Plan for Priority 6: Strengthening Governance and Institutional Capacity (photos by ADB).

Cover design by Nonie Villanueva.

Contents

Boxes

Acknowledgments

This guidance note was prepared by David Robinett, senior public management specialist (state-owned enterprise reform), under the auspices of the Asian Development Bank's State-Owned Enterprise Working Group, chaired by Bruno Carrasco, chief of the Governance Thematic Group, Sustainable Development and Climate Change Department.

Special thanks to the following staff for their advice and comments: Tahmeen Ahmad, Irum Ahsan, Ananya Basu, Alexandra Pamela Chiang, Gia Heeyoung Hong, Srinivasan Janardanam, Mary Kim, Yashna Shrawani, Lei Lei Song, and Adrian Torres. We would also like to thank the following for their support: Hyun Chang Park, Aly Tagumpay Escandor, Toni Figurasin, and Ashwath Dasarathy.

Abbreviations

ADB	Asian Development Bank
CSO	community service obligation
DMC	developing member country
IED	Independent Evaluation Department
OECD	Organisation for Economic Co-operation and Development
OP6	Operational Plan for Priority 6: Strengthening Governance and Institutional Capacity
RRP	report and recommendation of the President
PBL	policy-based lending
PPP	public–private partnership
RoE	return on equity
SDP	Sector Development Program
SOE	state-owned enterprise
TA	technical assistance

About This Guidance Note

Strategy 2030 and Operational Priority 6 commits the Asian Development Bank (ADB) to support state-owned enterprise (SOE) reform in its developing member countries (DMCs)[1]. This note is designed to help guide ADB staff in their work with SOEs, including in sovereign projects and policy-based loans (PBLs) and through technical assistance (TA). It reviews the significance of SOEs in Asia and the Pacific, the role of SOE reform in ADB's strategy, and related requirements for sovereign projects.

The guidance note addresses SOE challenges and areas of focus at the project level as well as in PBLs and sector development programs that combine policy-based and project lending. In addition, the note provides additional resources for staff working on SOE reform and briefly reviews the history of ADB's engagement with SOEs.

Although intended for ADB staff, this note may also be of use to DMC officials and SOE boards and management interested in SOE reform, in which case its most effective use would be in conjunction with other materials cited herein.

.

---

[1] ADB. 2019. *Strategy 2030 Operational Plan for Priority 6: Strengthening Governance and Institutional Capacity, 2019–2024.* Manila. https://www.adb.org/documents/strategy-2030-op6-governance.

Introduction

State-owned enterprises (SOEs) have long played an important role in developing economies of Asia and the Pacific. They remain dominant in areas with some of the highest development impact: energy, water, and transport, including passenger rail, ports, and airports. In many Asia and Pacific economies, SOEs are either the primary or sole provider of these vital goods and services, or the key counterpart/s of service delivery through contracting with the private sector or public–private partnerships (PPPs). Globally, SOEs account for 55% of infrastructure investment in middle- and lower-income economies.[2]

State-owned banks and financial institutions also make up a large part of the financial systems in Asia and the Pacific, holding 40% or more of banking system assets in a number of countries. SOEs, financial and nonfinancial, also account for some of world's largest firms and are major issuers of securities. The 2,000 largest SOEs have $45 trillion in assets and more than $7 trillion in debt, much of which are traded in the global bond market and include many of the largest publicly listed companies in Asia and the Pacific.[3]

SOEs hold significant public assets, and dividends can be a key source of public revenue. At the same time, SOEs to the national debt. If poorly managed, they can also impose a serious fiscal drain if governments are required to provide financial support through ongoing equity injections, loans, or subsidies. Overall, SOE debt can be as high as 50% of overall public sector debt, and as much as 20% of GDP in some countries. Ongoing spending related to SOEs can easily be from 1% to 3% of GDP, while well-managed state assets can contribute a similar amount in public revenue.[4]

The Asian Development Bank (ADB) has always worked with SOEs in its developing member countries (DMCs), and SOE reform remains an important part of ADB's strategy. This includes substantial operational work in the energy, water, transport, and financial sectors and sometimes in other sectors such as agriculture and information and communications technology. ADB also supports broader SOE reform and related sector reform through its policy-based lending (PBL) and technical assistance (TA). Over the years, SOE-linked lending has averaged about 25% of ADB's annual loans and grants. Much of this lending benefits from sovereign guarantees provided by DMC governments—which is the focus of this guidance note. ADB also makes loans directly to more commercial SOEs without a guarantee, primarily through its Private Sector Operations Department. This lending will be the focus of a forthcoming guidance note, as will cases in which the Private Sector Operations Department works jointly with ADB's regional departments to provide finance to SOEs.

---

[2] World Bank. 2017. *Who Sponsors Infrastructure Projects? Disentangling Public and Private Contributions.* Washington, DC.
[3] International Monetary Fund. 2020. *Fiscal Monitor.* Washington, DC.
[4] See footnote 2.

What Are State-Owned Enterprises?

ADB defines SOEs as legal entities established to undertake commercial activities and owned fully or largely by the sovereign.[5] The Organisation for Economic Co-operation and Development (OECD) uses a similar definition, a "corporate entity recognised by national law as an enterprise, and in which the state exercises ownership."[6] The SOE should have a distinct legal personality from government ministries or other governmental bodies. These include entities with the same legal form as enterprises in the private sector, such as limited liability companies and corporations. It also includes "statutory corporation," which are SOEs founded under their own act that have some revenue-earning functions.

As an enterprise, an SOE is distinct from other government agencies that are either regulatory in nature or provide a public good, for example air-traffic control or funding scientific research. It is also distinguished from state-owned schools and medical facilities, though some of the issues and good practices discussed here may be relevant to such bodies.

SOEs can be owned solely by a national government, or a provincial or municipal government. They may occasionally have multiple government owners, for example an urban transit system with national and municipal ownership, or an international pipeline owned by multiple governments of multiple nations. They may also have private investors, for example through listing on a stock exchange, or strategic investment by a private fund or company. In some cases, another SOE or a state-linked investment fund or financial institution may be an investor, either from the same or another country. This kind of cross-state-ownership has become increasingly prevalent as state-linked pension funds and sovereign wealth funds have grown and large SOEs have become increasingly multinational.

"Owned largely by the sovereign" implies 50% or more direct ownership. However, indirect ownership through other SOEs and state investors should also be taken into account. As should "golden shares," special rights sometimes found in company charters and laws give the state special veto powers over major decisions, even when they have less than 50% ownership.

---

[5] ADB. 2018. *State-Owned Enterprise Engagement and Reform: Thematic Evaluation.* Manila.
[6] OECD. 2015. *OECD Guidelines on Corporate Governance of State-Owned Enterprises.* Paris.

ADB's Strategy for State-Owned Enterprises

Strategy 2030 commits ADB to supporting SOE reform in its DMCs. It confirms the importance of this reform in lower, lower-middle, and upper middle-income economies and in small island developing states, as well as the importance of SOEs in providing many essential services in DMCs. Under Strategy 2030, ADB will work to improve SOE financial management capacity and internal governance. A primary goal of these reforms is to allow SOEs to access finance on commercial terms. In other words, the SOE has to be as attractive an investment as a credit-worthy private sector company, hence it should be comparable in terms of financial viability and also corporate governance, which impacts the ability of the SOE to credibly repay creditors and is essential for the SOE to attract equity investment. More broadly, Strategy 2030 supports policy and regulatory reform to ensure sustainable and effective service delivery.

Operational Plan for Priority 6: Strengthening Governance and Institutional Capacity (OP6) in Strategy 2030 goes into more detail on the importance of SOEs in DMCs and the SOE reform that the ADB will support. It confirms the importance of SOEs for service delivery and the goal of attracting commercial finance. OP6 also notes the potential fiscal impact SOEs can have, either as a source of revenue through dividends and taxes, or as a source of expenditures, through various subsidies and other state support. SOE debts can also be a significant source of contingent liabilities for governments, with implications for financial and debt sustainability.

Under OP6, ADB will support improvements to corporate governance and other steps to improve commercial orientation for SOEs. These include corporatization, that is converting the SOE to a company with the legal form similar to a private company, encouraging capital market access and equity investment, and shedding non-core assets.

It emphasizes ADB's support for the prudent disinvestment of state assets, where appropriate, and improving the governance and regulation of sectors where SOEs are predominant. In some cases, this can include exposing SOEs to greater competition. Critically, OP6 highlights the importance of the state measuring SOE performance, holding SOEs accountable for that performance, and improving how the state makes other major decisions in SOEs. To be successful, this reform should be underpinned by strong government ownership and support for relevant reforms.

ADB's work on SOEs is coordinated by the bank's SOE Working Group. Established in 2016, in phase 1 of its operations, the working group focused on knowledge sharing, data collection, and supporting the now mandatory identification of all projects and programs with SOEs. It also oversaw the development of a database on 10 years of SOE engagement that has now been integrated into ADB's e-Operations platform. The working group has now entered phase 2, building on phase 1 to directly support ADB's operational work with SOEs.

Challenges and Reforms for State-Owned Enterprises

Any enterprise in which the managers and owners are not the same can have agency problems, particularly when the managers may have more information about the enterprise than the owners and may act in their own interest, rather than in that of the owners.[7] In larger enterprises with many shareholders, tools that help manage these problems include modern corporate governance and the related areas of company law, corporate reporting, internal controls, and securities regulation.

SOEs face all of these potential problems, which may be compounded by the nature of their ownership. The state acts on behalf of the people through government. In practice for SOEs, these shareholder functions may be exercised by one or more ministries and/or other government agencies. This may lead to a complex agency chain wherein instead of a simple conflict between management and shareholders, there are conflicts among the broader general interests, the viability of the SOE, and various political and other interests held at different points in the agency chain.

In practice, SOE challenges tend to manifest themselves in the following ways:

- **Multiple objectives and mandates.** The SOE may have a mix of formal and informal goals and targets beyond profitability and providing their primary good or service. These may not be transparent, measured effectively, or fully or even partially funded.

- **Diffuse and weak accountability.** Various parts of the government may have responsibility over the SOE or ability to influence the SOE. At the same time, there may be no clear responsibility in ensuring that the SOE stays financially viable or maintains good corporate governance. When one body is responsible for the SOE, say a ministry, this responsibility may be exercised in a way that is unclear, ad hoc, opaque, conflicted in the objectives of the SOEs, and/or lacking relevant skills. All this creates conditions for substantial political influence.

- **Unlevel playing field with the private sector.** SOEs often have both advantages in terms of subsidies and other government favors, but also the penalties noted above. They may also have special rules in terms of governance, taxation, regulation, and other areas. In many cases, these reduce accountability, competition, and performance. A core problem: they often do not face the same penalties for persistent loss-making than that of private sector enterprises and managers because they can anticipate financial support from the state, state-linked financial institutions, or other SOEs.

- **High levels of opacity.** SOEs often do not meet the same requirements for disclosure and transparency as that of large, privately-owned companies with multiple shareholders, even though the public should be interested in their performance. Government decision-making in SOEs and the overall performance of the state-owned sector are also typically not disclosed or disclosed poorly.

---

[7] An agency problem—also known as a principal–agent problem—involves the presence of imperfect information, an agent (i.e., management) that is supposed to act in the interest of a principal (shareholders) may instead be tempted to act in their own interest.

- **Poor SOE governance.** In addition to, and because of, the challenges noted above, other elements of SOE governance may be weak. Board members may come primarily from the government and lack relevant skills and experience. Audit and other board committees may be absent, as will performance incentives. Management and employees may be governed by civil service norms. Critically, politicians and policymakers may make decisions at various levels in the SOE in a way that tends to undermine performance.

Box 1:   References and Resources for State-Owned Enterprise Reform

OECD Guidelines on Corporate Governance of State-Owned Enterprises (2015)
The international benchmark on SOE governance and reform from the OECD. Endorsed by the members of the OECD, the guidelines were also developed and revised with substantial input from Asian DMCs, including through consultations at the OECD in Paris and through the Asia Network on Corporate Governance of State-Owned Enterprises.

State-Owned Enterprise Engagement and Reform: Thematic Evaluation (2018)
A review of the ADB's work with SOEs by the Independent Evaluation Department (IED), its findings are described in Box 2.

Corporate Governance of State-Owned Enterprises: A Toolkit (2014)
This World Bank toolkit builds on years of global engagement in DMCs. It includes in-depth guidance on both national and SOE-specific reforms.

Asia Network on Corporate Governance of State-Owned Enterprises
This Network meets annually to discuss SOE reform issues and includes representatives from most Asian DMCs. Organized by the OECD with the support of the Korea Institute of Public Finance and ADB, the OECD and the Network have also produced a number of publications on SOE reform.

SOE Database in ADB e-Operations
Ten years of SOE data are embedded in the ADB's e-Operations platform covering 2010–2020. Through the SOE tagging process, this database is continually updated as new ADB projects with SOEs are undertaken. Reports from the database can be generated by the ADB Information and Technology Department.

Held by the Visible Hand: The Challenge of SOE Corporate Governance for Emerging Markets (2006)
This short paper from the World Bank gives a quick introduction to SOE challenges and reforms.

Public Commercial Assets: The Hidden Goldmine (2020)
This ADB Governance Brief provides the basic steps in professionalizing the state's ownership role, setting up a specialized ownership entity, and introducing two-sided balance sheets for public commercial assets.

Labor Issues in Infrastructure Reform: A Toolkit (2004)
This toolkit by the Public-Private Infrastructure Advisory Facility and World Bank gives in-depth guidance on how to manage SOE labor restructuring, including identifying surplus labor, handling severance, and helping to find new employment opportunities.

Finding Balance (2019 and earlier)
This series of reports from ADB's Private Sector Development Initiative benchmarks SOEs across Pacific economies and provides reform advice.

Source: Compiled by the authors.

Over the last 2 decades, modern SOE reform has developed to directly address these challenges. It borrows from the corporate governance of listed companies and adds good practices specifically for SOEs. These include (i) clarifying, accounting, and paying for non-commercial mandates—typically called community service or public service obligations (CSOs); (2) strengthening how the state acts as a sharehEolder, building accountability into this function, and focusing who carries it out; (iii) removing legal distinctions and separating policy, regulation, and ownership; (iv) encouraging a level playing field with the private sector; and (v) making SOEs comparable to leading private sector companies in terms of transparency and governance. Strong evidence is now available showing that these improvements to SOE governance increase SOE financial performance, service delivery, and fiscal impact.[8] Box 1 provides additional references on modern SOE reform.

---

[8]   For SOE-specific reforms, see L.A. Andrés, J.L. Guasch, S. López Azumendi. 2011. Governance in State-Owned Enterprises Revisited: The Cases of Water and Electricity in Latin America and the Caribbean. *Policy Research Working Paper*. No. 5747. Washington, DC: The World Bank; and A. Baum et al. 2019. "Governance and State-Owned Enterprises: How Costly is Corruption?" *IMF Working Papers*. No. 19/253. Washington, DC: The International Monetary Fund. For the benefits of broader SOE reforms and fiscal impact, see D. Detter. 2020. Public Commercial Assets: The Hidden Goldmine. *The Governance Brief*. Issue 40. Manila: Asian Development Bank. For the benefits of corporate governance reform more generally in DMCs, see S. Claessens and B. Yurtoglu. 2012. *Corporate Governance and Development—An Update*. Washington, DC: Global Corporate Governance Forum and International Finance Corporation.

ADB Investment Projects with State-Owned Enterprises

To implement Strategy 2030 and ensure development impact, all ADB projects with SOEs have minimum requirements. The report and recommendation of the President (RRP)—the main document describing an ADB project—should describe ADB's overall engagement and reform plan, if any, for the specific entity. In addition, the RRP should note the "(i) key governance and reform issues which need to be addressed for the particular SOE within the broader sector context (e.g., internal governance, financial reporting, internal audit, and disclosure) and (ii) explicit details on how the project components contribute to the overall medium- to long-term SOE reform agenda.[9]

In practice, these requirements for the RRP apply to both loans and grants. They imply that the SOE should be clearly introduced in the rationale of the RRP and its governance challenges presented there. The RRP should also present reform that goes beyond the immediate needs of the project and contribute to the longer-term viability of the SOE.

In these projects, an SOE is typically an executing or implementing agency. SOE governance- and reform-related due diligence will be required to confirm the (i) financial viability of the SOE and (ii) financial management capabilities. Two ADB documents explain how to conduct this due diligence: *Financial Analysis and Evaluation Technical Guidance Note* (October 2019) and *Financial Management Technical Guidance Note* (May 2015). State-owned banks and financial institutions that will act as financial intermediaries have a separate guidance note for financial due diligence.[10]

When resulting recommendations are included in an effective reform plan and key loan and grant covenants and implemented by the SOE and the state owner, these help to ensure that the SOE will remain viable and reduce the likelihood that an adverse financial or governance event will undermine the development impact of the ADB project.

Supporting State-Owned Enterprise Reform in ADB Projects

Listed in the next page are the main areas for which SOE reform should be considered as part of an ADB project. This list does not supersede or replace the required financial due diligence, and such due diligence is a good way to start to identify effective SOE reform. However, SOE reform often goes beyond financial due diligence into

---

[9] ADB Strategy, Policy and Partnerships Department. 2018. Alignment of Projects with Strategy 2030–Description in the Report and Recommendation of the President. Memorandum. 13 November.
[10] ADB. 2018. *Financial Due Diligence for Financial Intermediaries. Technical Guidance Note*, Manila.

other areas of SOE corporate governance. Appendix 1 gives a list of additional information to gather about the SOE to facilitate effective reform.

To implement SOE reform, the SOE and the government often need additional expertise; ADB TA can be effective here. The references in Box 1 give more in-depth guidance on SOE reform. This includes *Corporate Governance of State-Owned Enterprises: A Toolkit,* including Chapters 3–7 and Appendixes C, D, and E.

REVENUE AND SERVICE REQUIREMENTS. The financial analysis required as part of due diligence will give projections for the viability of the SOE. Any number of factors can impact its recent and projected financial performance. For many SOEs, one of the most important is the tariffs (prices) that it can charge end-users. These may be capped, either through formal regulation or through informal government pressure. It is also common to have different rates for different end-users, for example, through multi-tiered pricing, usually to make the good or service cheaper for lower-income households. There may also be issues with collection from some end-users.

Overall, tariffs should be high enough to ensure sufficient revenue for the long-term viability of the SOE. For medium- to longer-term SOE reform, they should be set in an objective manner, preferably by an independent authority, and take full account of variable costs, as well as depreciation, operations, and maintenance. When needed, collection rates should also be improved. There should be some benchmarking to ensure that costs are reasonable. Restructuring and other steps may be needed to bring costs down, as discussed below. When below-cost provision is required, a transparent, predictable, and long-term subsidy should be provided. This formal system for CSOs should be linked to output and other measures of service delivery.

FINANCIAL STRUCTURE. High levels of debt relative to income and or equity may also undermine the financial viability of the SOE. If an immediate crisis is not foreseen, the SOE would still need to move away from net borrowing, except for investment purposes, and move to net profitability to build up equity and or pay down debt. If the levels of debt are too high, then debt may need to be restructured, and/or equity injected. In both scenarios, government commitment is required.

The other SOE reforms discussed in this section can help to build up longer-term creditworthiness, bring down interest rates, and increase access to private sector borrowing. A credible plan to implement these reforms should be paired with any government financial relief. The ADB publication *The Bankable SOE* (January 2021) has more on how to improve SOE creditworthiness.

MAINTENANCE OF ASSETS. To preserve the value of its assets, including those developed under the project, the SOE should take account of depreciation and ongoing operation and maintenance expenses. It should be able to cover these expenses and devote enough resources to preserve physical assets. These asset lifecycle issues should be considered at the design stage for the project and when it is under preparation.[11] In addition, effective asset maintenance requires proper accounting treatment and proper internal controls, as discussed below. Additional steps may be required to ensure that resources are available. This includes preserving financial viability as noted above and binding commitments in loan covenants to undertake sufficient operation and maintenance spending. Asset preservation may also take other steps, such as setting up a reserve fund to ensure resources will be available for future maintenance.

Some state assets may be especially vulnerable to natural disasters, climate change, or other kinds of risk. Disaster risk management plans should be developed in these cases. Insurance options should also be explored.[12]

---

[10]   Quality Infrastructure Investment Partnership. 2019. "G20 Principles for Quality Infrastructure Investment." Washington, DC.
[11]   ADB. "Insuring State Assets in Samoa and the Pacific." Manila. Forthcoming.

INTERNAL AUDIT AND CONTROLS. The required financial management analysis will include risks and recommendations related to internal audit and other aspects of internal controls. These functions should be in place and any identified risks managed appropriately. For medium- and longer-term SOE reform, the SOE should have an independent internal audit function that reports to the board, preferably an audit committee with qualified, independent members. The internal audit function should ensure compliance with and effectiveness of the SOE's internal controls.

EXTERNAL AUDIT AND CORPORATE REPORTING. The required financial management analysis will also include risks and recommendations for external audit and corporate reporting. At a minimum, the SOE should be subject to regular audit by a capable government auditor. For medium- and longer-term SOE reform, the SOE and its financial statements should also be subject to external audit by a qualified audit firm. Best practice is for the governmental auditor to focus on use of public funds and SOE performance and service delivery.

The SOE will need to have current financial statements available for the financial due diligence, which also includes a review of accounting practices and capabilities. Going beyond these for medium- and longer-term SOE reform, the SOE should produce financial statements using International Financial Reporting Standards. They should also disclose key nonfinancial information, including on non-state shareholders and ownership, board members, and top management and policies toward accounting and auditing, ethics, and risk, and transactions with other SOEs and the government, including material arears and receivables.

PERFORMANCE MANAGEMENT. The SOE should have key performance indicators. These may set by the owner, and—for measures of service delivery or in the context of sector regulation—possibly by the regulator or policymaking ministry. For medium- and longer-term SOE reform, independent experts may be involved in setting targets and assessing performance, and feedback may be provided by end-users on service delivery. These mechanisms can also help compensate for limited institutional capacity on behalf of state owners.

Return on equity (RoE) or a close equivalent measure, such as economic value added or return on assets,[13] should be one of the indicators.[14] This ensures efficient use of the SOE's assets and a return to state owners and helps impose discipline on the SOE's management. This is complemented by a CSO system that covers the costs of policy mandates and by dividend targets that ensure regular payments to state and other shareholders. RoE should be benchmarked against comparable industries and take into account the typical source of finance for the SOE. For example, public transit or water, which may rely largely on concessional finance, would typically have a lower target RoE than shipping or electricity transmission, which may have better access to commercial finance. Oil, gas, and other natural resource providers would tend to have the highest RoE targets.

BOARD AND MANAGEMENT QUALITY. SOE board members and senior management should be qualified and able to act in the interest of the SOE. In practice, too many SOE board members and senior managers are chosen for political reasons or to preserve government control, at the expense of SOE performance. They may not meet the qualifications of their equivalents in the private sector, and they may facilitate political interference in the operations of the SOE. For medium- and longer-term SOE reform, no minister or member of Parliament or equivalent should serve on the board, most board members should not be civil servants, and all should have relevant professional or commercial backgrounds. Board selection should be transparent and based on skill and the needs of the SOE. Multiple board members should be independent of company management and the government. The chief executive officer (CEO) should be chosen solely based on professional qualifications, preferably by the board.

---

[13]   D. Detter and S. Fölster. 2015. *Public Wealth of Nations: How Management of Public Assets Can Boost or Bust Economic Growth.* London: UK Palgrave Macmillan.

[14]   OECD. 2019. *Ownership and Governance of State-Owned Enterprises: A Compendium of National Practices.* Paris.

The internal auditor and external auditor should report to independent members of the board, preferably to an audit committee with at least one member who has expertise in finance and accounting. Independent board members should also approve the pay of the CEO, and the board should carry out other functions comparable to boards in the private sector. This includes CEO selection and overseeing the SOE's strategy, risk management, performance management, ethics and compliance, and other key areas.

HUMAN RESOURCES AND RESTRUCTURING. An SOE that is performing poorly financially may have too many staff that have been hired for reasons other than ensuring SOE performance, and/or too many activities outside its core areas of service delivery. Restructuring in this case will require identification of less-qualified or unnecessary staff. It may also require the closing or sale of parts of the SOE that do not contribute to its core functions or service delivery. For staff who leave the SOE, provisions should be made for pension obligations and maintenance of income until new employment can be found, and this may need to come from the government or state shareholder. *Labor Issues in Infrastructure Reform: A Toolkit* provides additional guidance on SOE restructuring (see Box 1).

Although the SOE may be overstaffed, the staff may be underpaid. Restrictive rules for pay and human resources based on public sector norms may be in place; these can limit the ability of the SOE to compete with the private sector or reach comparably performance benchmarks. Medium- and longer-term SOE reform will require moving toward private sector practices for pay and performance management.

STATE OVERSIGHT AND PROFESSIONALISM. Many of the challenges SOEs face ultimately come from how the state carries out its ownership functions. Medium- and long-term SOE reform should aim for minimum political interference; and sufficient autonomy for SOE boards and management, with the state shareholder exercising their rights through normal channels used by shareholders in private sector companies, such as approving board members and major decisions in the general meeting of shareholders. The state's shareholder and ownership functions should be carried out in a professional manner, preferably through a specialized entity and the state should have the capability of overseeing SOE and its portfolio of state assets.

Box 2:   ADB's Engagement with State-Owned Enterprises Before and After Strategy 2030

The 2018 publication *State-Owned Enterprise Engagement and Reform: Thematic Evaluation* by the Independent Evaluation Department (IED) confirms ADB's long-standing engagement on and commitment to SOE reform. However, it also shows limited support for the more effective types of modern SOE reform. For example, ADB has supported broader legal reform to bolster the private sector to improve public sector management and fiscal performance. Yet, it involves only small components of SOE reform or had an indirect impact on SOE governance.

ADB has had some success in supporting the corporatization, privatization, and closing of lossmaking SOEs, but this tends to be inherently challenging and some attempted or proposed privatizations and closings have failed. The bank has supported broader sector reform, for example helping establish an independent regulator and making SOE pricing more tied to cost and sustainability. However, as noted here and other IED reports, it has pursued this reform in a limited number of countries and instances. Finally, the ADB has supported SOE reform in its investment projects, but usually in the context of the project, and has done less to support wider reform for the SOE that would contribute to its longer-term sustainability.

continued on next page

Box 2:   *continued*

The evaluation confirms that those areas of SOE reform that have often been identified as the most important and effective have received limited support.[a] This includes strengthening government oversight of SOEs, SOE accountability, and SOE boards.

A separate analysis of ADB's SOE engagements for the previous decade largely confirms the IED's findings. Reforms related to the project and required financial due diligence tended to be more common; these ncluded financial management, human resources and staff capacity, and transparency and disclosure. Broader legal reforms also tended to be more common, and included some reform to SOE's regulated prices and other sector reforms. However, some of the most important SOE governance reforms, including those involving SOE boards and how the state exercises ownership and SOE autonomy, were some of the least common. About 47% of projects had no SOE reform or limited SOE reform, while only 29% had more extensive SOE reform.

Type of SOE Reform Analysis	% Age of Projects
Financial Management	54
Human Resource	52
Other Reforms	49
Legal & Regulatory Framework	44
Transparency & Accountability	42
Privatization & PPPs	35
Software (ERP/MIS)	25
Financial Restructuring	19
Ownership & Autonomy	16
Board Structure	15

One persistent area of strength has been the ADB's TA. The ADB has used its TA to both support reform linked to specific projects and policy-based lending. TA has also been used to support reform when no lending is required, and this included wider sector and national SOE reform.

ADB's Support for SOE Reform since 2018

In the wake of the IED report and to implement Strategy 2030, ADB has made key changes in how it addresses SOE reform. Work with SOEs is now tagged and tracked to facilitate information sharing and learning on SOE related work. All projects with SOEs should now address governance challenges and reforms options. There has been an increase in projects that include both sector and SOE reform, with multiple such projects being prepared in 2020. There has also been more TA for SOE reform, including to a number of DMCs that are looking to make bigger reforms in how their government oversees SOEs and holds them accountable, including setting up or strengthening specialized agencies and holding companies for SOE oversight and commercialization.

---

[a] See the references in Box 1 and footnote 4.

continued on next page

Box 2:   *continued*

Under the leadership of ADB's SOE Working Group, there has been renewed emphasis on operations and taking a One ADB approach to preparing SOEs for commercial borrowing and better understanding "hybrid" lending options that mix sovereign and nonsovereign elements. A study, *The Bankable SOE* is forthcoming, as well as a guidance note on nonsovereign and hybrid lending to SOEs. Another area being developed builds on the need for greater resilience and climate proofing of state assets including integrating insurance options for state assets, especially in the Pacific, where vulnerability to damage from disasters has been magnified by climate change. Greater emphasis has also been placed on staff training and awareness-raising and supporting ADB staff in their work on SOE reform.

Source: Authors.

ADB Policy-Based and Programmatic Lending

ADB's PBL can provide an effective tool to support SOE reform. It can be used to support SOE-specific reform; support such reform in multiple SOEs; and strengthen SOE governance at a national, provincial, or municipal level, or for a particular sector.

Policy actions under a PBL may include government commitment to legal and regulatory changes, new or changes to government policies, other government decisions, and SOE-level policies and decisions. The legal basis for SOE governance and policymaking varies across countries. However, it is always important to have clear and concrete government commitment. As with project lending, this reform is often best supported by TA. The references in Box 1 provide more in-depth guidance on SOE reform. For national and sector reform, this includes *Corporate Governance of State-Owned Enterprises: A Toolkit,* Chapters 2 through 5 and Appendixes A and B.

Professionalizing state oversight. The most effective way to create political insulation, professionalize state oversight of SOEs, and promote SOE governance[15] is to create a specialized ownership entity–either an agency, investment fund, or a holding company.[16] A growing number of Asian economies have introduced or are considering the creation of such entities. A professionalized ownership entity can effectively carry out the state shareholder function while focusing on returns for the shareholder and still ensure that the key service mandates can be met. Such an entity can be created at the national, provincial, or municipal level. It can also be created for a subset of assets, such as state-owned financial institutions. A ministry devoted to overseeing SOE governance and performance may also be effective, but should ensure political insulation for its SOEs. The government should also have the capacity to monitor performance, including of the broader SOE portfolio and of the specialized entity when present.

Part of this process includes understanding the extent of the state's commercial assets, providing an initial valuation, updating the registrar of the state's commercial assets, and ultimately creating balance sheets that show both the state's commercial assets and related liabilities held under the respective ownership entity. By introducing assets as well as liabilities, these balance sheets can help facilitate needed investment, and better account for asset maintenance and depreciation, as noted above. *Public Commercial Assets: The Hidden Goldmine* gives additional guidance on creating such entities and developing two-sided balance sheets.

A clear regulatory and legal basis for SOEs and state oversight should be in place, including for the various areas noted here. This may include an *ownership policy* that sets out the broader goals of state ownership and provides greater detail on how the state carries out its ownership functions.

Accounting for and financing policy mandates. To help guide SOE governance and oversight, many countries divide SOEs into two categories: (i) commercial in nature, and (ii) policy-oriented. In practice some policy-oriented "SOEs," for example, those that provide public goods or regulatory functions, are effectively

---

[15]   D. Detter. 2020. Public Commercial Assets: the Hidden Goldmine. *The Governance Brief.* Issue 40. Manila: Asian Development Bank.

[16]   OECD. 2015. *OECD Guidelines on Corporate Governance of State-Owned Enterprises.* Paris.

corporatized government agencies and do not fall under standard definitions of an SOE. Other SOEs, both those more policy-oriented and those considered more commercial, will often have service-delivery targets and obligations. Up to a point, this may be consistent with a commercial orientation. Private sector companies also want to satisfy their consumers and end-users. As these services may be essential in nature, including water, electricity, public transit, access to finance, and other vital services, it is not unusual for the government to want to ensure that they are supplied in a reliable manner.

However, the SOEs' policy mandates can become problematic when they are underfunded, nontransparent, or ad hoc. SOEs should not be asked to do things that fall outside their mandate or without a clear process behind it. If such a mandate is necessary, a transparent, predictable, and long-term subsidy should be provided. This formal system for CSOs should be linked to output and other measures of service delivery. As noted, independent experts may be involved in assessing performance, and feedback may be provided by end-users on service delivery. When such a system is in place, it facilitates better performance management, including achieving standard industry measures of service delivery and hitting reasonable RoE targets.

In the longer-term, commercial SOEs can be gradually freed of these requirements. Certain commodity-based or in-kind subsidies may also be replaced by targeted cash transfers or similar programs, which can reduce SOE mandates and the government's overall fiscal commitments and bring multiple economic benefits.[17] As discussed next, the private sector may also be brought in to play a greater role in providing some of these services.

Legal status and level playing field with the private sector. The SOE should have an autonomous legal status separate from the government administration, with its own board and management. Preferably, it should be a company or corporation under the same law(s) used by private sector companies. The SOE may have a complex set of advantages and disadvantages compared to private sector enterprises. The reforms listed above and their impacts can help remove these distortions. These include political insulation, adopting private sector norms for governance, and introducing CSO systems and RoE and dividend targets.

Reforms should ensure that the SOE is subject to equal treatment in regulation and law more generally. This is one of the reasons why the ownership entity should be separate from policymaking and regulatory parts of the government. The SOE should also have the same tax treatment as private sector entities and also be treated the same under competition law, when relevant. In the most advanced cases, SOEs and private firms could compete to provide certain services.[18]

Privatization and private sector engagement. The ADB has supported privatization for many years and attracting private sector capital and engagement to SOEs is emphasized by Strategy 2030. However, privatization may not always be the best option for an SOE, and DMC government commitment is crucial. Successful privatization will require many of the steps noted above: (i) moving to the same legal status and treatment as private sector companies; (ii) limiting or removing policy mandates and finding alternatives if needed; (iii) removing links to the government and moving to private sector norms of governance; and (iv) preparing high-quality audited financial statements and providing other information to bidders and investors.

Each of these steps is essential for companies to be fully privatized. Such a process should be conducted in a highly transparent and competitive manner. Unless the value of underlying assets is clear, restructuring may be needed before the transaction takes place, and stakeholder considerations should be addressed, as described

---

[17]   D. Jishnu. 2005. Reassessing Conditional Cash Transfer Programs. *The World Bank Research Observer* (20) 1. Washinglton, DC: The World bank. pp. 57–80.

[18]   For additional steps to enhance the level playing field with the private sector in DMCs with more advanced SOE reform, see OECD. 2012. *Competitive Neutrality: Maintaining a Level Playing Field between Public and Private Business.* Paris.

above. In cases where the new owner may restructure, commitments to employees and other stakeholders should still be taken into account, and provisions made as part of the privatization process.

When government is going to retain some ownership, all the SOE reforms noted above are important, and the state's position and voting rights should be executed in a professional and objective manner. The interest of minority shareholders should be taken into account. This requires high levels of board and management quality as well as specific steps to protect minority shareholders. Section IV of the *OECD Guidelines on Corporate Governance of State-Owned Enterprises (2015)* and Chapter 8 of the *Corporate Governance of State-Owned Enterprises: A Toolkit* provide additional guidance on effective treatment of non-state shareholders.

SOEs that have been reformed are generally in a better position to effectively deal with the private sector on a professional and arm's length basis. This includes access to finance, as well as procurement and outsourcing. Contracting out more functions with the private sector can improve SOE efficiency, and, if the SOE has a significant presence in the economy, encourage private sector development. However, such contracting should be transparent and avoid conflicts of interest.

Sector Reform PBLs and Sector Development Programs

PBLs can provide an effective way to deal with sector issues that go beyond a single project. Sector Development Programs (SDP) combine PBL lending and policy actions with investment project lending. They can be used to address both wider policy issues and capacity building at a range of levels, as well as fund needed investment. For SOEs, they are especially relevant in the energy, finance, transport, and water sectors. Broader sector reform, including of SOEs, also creates a more effective enabling environment for ADB investment projects in that sector.

Sector PBLs and SDPs can be used to support any of the reforms noted above for one or more SOEs in a specific sector. They can also be used to strengthen regulatory frameworks for the sector in ways that make SOEs more efficient and improve service delivery and to address sector-specific issues for these SOEs. These frameworks can also incorporate measures of performance management and can include CSO systems or close equivalents. Overall goals of reform include maintaining minimum service standards and ensuring financial sustainability for the regulated entities and service access for lower-income or isolated populations. It can also include encouraging private sector participation when appropriate for the sector.

When possible, policymaking, regulation, and carrying out the state's ownership functions should be separate functions. For example, in energy this would mean a ministry for policy functions, an independent agency for energy regulation, and a separate ownership entity for state-owned energy assets. This type of model is also applicable to finance, civil aviation, and telecommunications. In other sectors, establishing separate regulators may not be as common, but the regulatory framework should still seek to achieve some separation of general policy, setting regulated prices and other standards, and overseeing the commercial performance and governance of the SOE.

Conclusion

Building State-Owned Enterprise Reform into Projects and Programs

To build SOE reform into an ADB project, start at or before the concept stage. Learn what previous SOE reforms and TAs have been carried out in the relevant SOE or sector. Commit to a dialogue with the counterpart to establish the importance and usefulness of SOE reform, and find common ground on the reforms that will be supported. The concept paper should briefly introduce and describe the SOE and identify a few areas where reform may be needed. Next, use the financial due diligence, together with the questions in Appendix 1, to understand possible challenges in more detail and identify unforeseen challenges at the concept stage. The questions in Appendix 1 should be completed by a specialist familiar with accounting and auditing, corporate law, and/or SOE governance.

Based on these findings, use the advice in this note and, if needed, the references in Box 2, to develop proposed reforms. A similar approach can be used for PBLs and SDPs, along with the enterprise-specific questions in Appendix 1 for a few major SOEs or typical or representative SOEs. In each case, try to find a TA that can help the proposed reforms to be implemented. Broader discussions on national SOE reform should also be linked the country partnership strategy process, and when relevant included in the country partnership strategy.[19] Critically, substantial SOE reform will require a champion in the SOE or in government, and that champion should be supported through the ADB's engagement.

It may not be possible to address all the areas noted here, or all the potential weaknesses identified. At the project level, any weakness identified that could impact the execution, sustainability, or effectiveness of the project should be addressed. Additional SOE reform should be undertaken to improve the viability of the SOE beyond the project. As indicated in Strategy 2030, SOE reform should improve service delivery and move the SOE closer to accessing nonsovereign finance. For a PBL or SDP, policy actions should be consistent with the good practices described here and strengthen the performance and sustainability of a si14gnificant part of the state-owned sector. Importantly, broader SOE reform will also improve the quality and viability of investment projects later undertaken by the reformed SOEs.

Under the SOE Working Group, the ADB provides ongoing training and information sharing for staff and DMC officials on SOE reform. This training can provide greater comfort with the material presented here and new perspectives on SOE challenges and opportunities. Help is also available through the governance team in the ADB's Sustainable Development and Climate Change Department, either through ADB staff or recommended consultants. Bringing a specialist in early on for the project or program can be one of the best ways to enhance SOE reform. Appendix 2 contains sample terms of reference to (i) support governance reform at the project level, and (ii) help develop and implement policy actions for a PBL.

---

[19] ADB. 2018. *Management Response to Thematic Evaluation on State-Owned Enterprise Engagement and Reform.* Manila.

Appendix 1: Supplemental Questions for State-Owned Enterprise Due Diligence

A. Legal Form and Level Playing Field	Response
1. Does the SOE have legal autonomy from the government?	
2. Is it formed under the national company law or equivalent, its own act, or in another way?	
3. Is the SOE subject to the same requirements in terms of taxation, labor law, environmental regulation, and other areas as private sector enterprises?	
4. Is the SOE subject to sector regulation?	
5. Is sector regulation set independently from sector policy, for example by an independent body?	
6. Is it set separately from ownership decisions?	
7. Is there private sector participation in the sector?	

B. Ownership Arrangements and Political Insulation	Response
1. Does the SOE report to one or more ministries, government agencies, or other entities? Which ones?	
2. Which entity(ies) makes major decisions, like board nomination or appointment, approving major decisions like mergers or divestments, oversees performance management, etc.?	
3. Is the entity with primary responsibility for performing these functions for the SOE an agency, holding company, or other entity focused on acting as the state owner, or carrying out similar functions, and separate from policymaking ministries and sector regulators?	
4. Do those in the government and/or ownership entity responsible for overseeing SOE performance have the skills needed to evaluate SOE financial and nonfinancial reporting, board selection and performance, SOE strategy, and related areas?	
5. Can the management of the SOE make decisions, short of major changes in strategy or those that would affect the character of the SOE, without consulting the government (including government representatives on the board)?	
6. Is the management or board of the SOE subject to ongoing instructions from the government?	

continued on next page

C.	Mandates, Subsidies, and Community Service Obligations	Response
1.	Does the SOE receive subsidies from the government to cover its operating expenses?	
2.	If so, for how much and for what specific purpose(s)?	
3.	Are these subsidies provided under a formal public service or community service obligation system?	
4.	Are the subsidies clearly linked to output or other targets?	
5.	Are these subsidies transparent and disclosed to the public?	
6.	Is the SOE asked to take on special projects or assignments without being reimbursed for them?	
7.	Is there a formal process for these policy mandates and requests?	
8.	Are these requests in line with the competencies and mandate of the SOE?	

D.	Performance Management	Response
1.	Does the SOE have any "key performance indicators" or equivalent?	
2.	Are these developed as part of a formal performance agreement, such as a memorandum of understanding or statement of corporate intent?	
3.	Do performance metrics include a measure such as return on equity, return on capital employed, economic value added or a similar measure of profitability and asset management?	
4.	Do performance metrics include measures of service delivery?	
5.	Are some measures of minimum service delivery set by a regulator?	
6.	Is end-user feedback provided on service delivery?	

E.	Human Resources	Response
1.	Does the SOE have enough employees to carry out its activities? Too many?	
2.	Is it short on employees with certain skills or capabilities?	
3.	Is the pay of the SOE competitive with the private sector?	
4.	Is the pay of senior management linked to the performance of the SOE?	
5.	Overall, are human resource arrangements at the SOE closer to the civil service and/or government or the private sector?	

continued on next page

Appendix 1:   *continued*

F.	SOE Board and Management Quality	Response
1.	Are there members of the board that are independent of the SOE management and the government? Who are they?	
2.	Are there members of the board that have relevant commercial and sector experience?	
3.	Are there members of the board that have specialized skills, like accounting and auditing, or other relevant skills?	
4.	How are board members nominated and appointed?	
5.	Can serving board members help identify the skills needed for an incoming board member?	
6.	What is the process for choosing the CEO?	
7.	Does the board lead this process?	
8.	How is pay for the CEO determined?	
9.	Does the board lead this process?	
10.	What is the background of the CEO?	
11.	Does the board oversee or provide input into the SOE's strategy?	
12.	Does the CEO and management develop the SOE's strategy?	
13.	Does the board have an audit committee or other specialized committees?	
14.	Through a board committee or another mechanism, can independent member of the board provide input into and oversee key areas, such as audit, related-party transactions, and CEO pay?	

Appendix 2: Indicative Terms of Reference for State-Owned Enterprise Diagnostics

International State-Owned Enterprise Project and Sector Specialists

The SOE project and sector specialist will conduct a diagnostics of governance in or more SOEs in support of [ADB PROJECT OR TA] in [DMC NAME]. They will provide recommendations for SOE reform and support-related capacity building, working closely with [ADB DEPARTMENT] and counterparts to increase understanding and facilitate implementation of better SOE governance and performance. The consultant will carry out the following tasks:

- Collect quantitative and qualitative data on SOE governance, this includes data related to sector governance and regulation, SOE internal governance, transparency and disclosure, implicit and explicit public sector obligations, and related issues. The data collected should be consistent with Appendix 1 of *Guidance Note on State-Owned Enterprise Reform in Sovereign Projects and Programs,* ADB 2020 (the Guidance Note).

- Analyze and summarize findings from collected data and undertake gap and risk analysis in light of *Guidance Note on State-Owned Enterprise Reform in Sovereign Projects and Programs,* ADB 2020, and internationally-agreed standards including the Organisation for Economic Co-operation and Development (OECD) Guidelines on Corporate Governance of State-Owned Enterprises, the World Bank Corporate Governance of State-Owned Enterprises Toolkit, and other relevant standards, including for accounting and auditing.

- Interview DMC officials, SOE board members and management, and local stakeholders and experts in preparing diagnostics and in capacity building and effectively boost their understanding of relevant challenges and solutions.

- Develop appropriate and relevant recommendations to address SOE challenges, including in all areas as identified in the first bullet point. The primary focus should be SOE specific reforms but may also include recommendations for government regulation and policy, legal changes, and sector.

- If needed, conduct or facilitate consultations, dialogues, workshops, and other necessary activities with DMC government agencies, SOEs, the private sector, local and international experts and professionals, civil society and other development stakeholders, including to gather inputs and present and discuss results, findings, and recommendations in reports prepared under the TA.

- Conduct consultations and participate in discussions with relevant staff of ADB operations departments and resident missions on findings and recommendations of diagnostics and planned capacity building, in order to ensure that ADB is able to respond to emerging demands for SOE-related support from DMCs.

The qualifications for the consultant will include an advanced university degree in economics, accounting, business, law, public administration, or other related fields. The consultant should have at least 10 years of demonstrated skills and experience in SOE reforms and sufficient knowledge of the relevant international discourse in governance and institutional development, including the work of the OECD and relevant international financial institutions. He or she should have experience with DMCs and working closely with government officials, as well as officers and employees in SOEs. They should be comfortable working with SOEs in [RELEVANT SECTOR]. The consultant should also have excellent oral and written communication skills in English, strong analytical skills, and a proven track record in producing high-quality technical reports.

International State-Owned Enterprise Policy Specialists

The SOE policy specialist will support diagnostics on SOE governance in [DMC] and help identify sector and/or national level SOE reforms. They will also support capacity building in DMCs, working closely with counterparts to increase understanding and facilitate implementation of better SOE governance and performance. The consultant will carry out the following tasks:

- Collect quantitative and qualitative data on SOE governance, policy, law, regulation, and operational and financial performance. These include data related to sector governance and regulation, SOE internal governance, transparency and disclosure, access to private finance and private sector participation, implicit and explicit public sector obligations, and related public finance issues. [It also includes data related to broader public asset management, including state-owned real estate, and data at the provincial and subnational level.]

- Analyze and summarize findings from collected data and undertake gap and risk analysis in light of Guidance Note on State-Owned Enterprise Reform in Sovereign Projects and Programs, ADB 2020, and internationally-agreed standards including the Organisation for Economic Co-operation and Development (OECD) Guidelines on Corporate Governance of State-Owned Enterprises, the World Bank Corporate Governance of State-Owned Enterprises Toolkit, and other relevant standards, including for accounting and auditing.

- Interview DMC officials, SOE board members and management, and local stakeholders and experts in preparing diagnostics and in capacity building and effectively boost their understanding of relevant challenges and solutions.

- Develop appropriate and relevant recommendations to address SOE challenges, including in all areas as identified in the first bullet point. These may include recommendations for government regulation and policy, legal changes, and sector- and SOE-specific reforms.

- Conduct or facilitate consultations, dialogues, workshops and other necessary activities with DMC government agencies, SOEs, the private sector, local and international experts and professionals, civil society and other development stakeholders, including to gather inputs and present and discuss results, findings and recommendations in reports prepared under the TA.

- Conduct consultations and participate in discussions with relevant staff of ADB operations departments and resident missions on findings and recommendations of diagnostics and planned capacity building, in order to ensure that ADB is able to respond to emerging demands for SOE-related support from DMCs.

- Liaise closely with project management of the TA and relevant staff within the operational department and other ADB departments, as well as other consultants engaged under the TA, in the accomplishments of outlined outputs.

- Other activities as deemed necessary to successfully conduct the diagnostics and help build DMC capacity.

The qualifications for the consultant will include an advanced university degree in economics, accounting, business, law, public administration, or other related fields. The consultant should have at least 10 years of demonstrated skills and experience in SOE reforms and sufficient knowledge of the relevant international discourse in governance and institutional development, including the work of the OECD and relevant international financial institutions. He or she should have experience with DMCs and working closely with government officials, as well as officers and employees in SOEs. The consultant should also have excellent oral and written communication skills in English, strong analytical skills, and a proven track record in producing high-quality technical reports.

Bibliography

L.A. Andrés, J.L. Guasch, S. López Azumendi. 2011. "Governance in State-Owned Enterprises Revisited: The Cases of Water and Electricity in Latin America and the Caribbean." World Bank Working Paper, Washington, DC.

Asian Development Bank (ADB). 2018. "Alignment of Projects with Strategy 2030 – Description in the RRPs." Memorandum, 13 November.

———. 2018. Financial Due Diligence for Financial Intermediaries. Technical Guidance Note, Manila.

———. 2018. Management Response to Thematic Evaluation on State-Owned Enterprise Engagement and Reform. Manila.

———. 2018. State-Owned Enterprise Engagement and Reform: Thematic Evaluation. Manila.

———. 2019. Finding Balance 2019: Benchmarking the Performance of State-Owned Banks in the Pacific. Manila.

A. Baum, C. Hackney, P. Medas, M. Sy. 2019. "Governance and State-Owned Enterprises: How Costly is Corruption?" IMF Working Paper, Washington, DC.

S. Claessens and B. Yurtoglu. 2012. "Corporate Governance and Development: An Update. Global Corporate Governance Forum Focus. International Finance Corporation, Washington, DC.

D. Detter. 2019. "Public Commercial Assets: The Hidden Goldmine." Governance Brief. ADB Manila.

D. Detter and S. Fölster. 2015. Public Wealth of Nations: How Management of Public Assets Can Boost or Bust Economic Growth. London: UK Palgrave Macmillan.

D. Jishnu. 2005. "Reassessing Conditional Cash Transfer Programs." The World Bank Research Observer (Vol. 20), No. 1 (Spring 2005). pp. 57–80.

D. Robinett. 2006. Held by the Visible Hand: The Challenge of SOE Corporate Governance for Emerging Markets. World Bank. Washington DC.

International Monetary Fund. 2020. Fiscal Monitor. Washington, DC.

Organisation for Economic Co-operation and Development (OECD). 2012. Competitive Neutrality: Maintaining a Level Playing Field between Public and Private Business. Paris.

———. 2015. OECD Guidelines on Corporate Governance of State-Owned Enterprises OECD 2015. Paris.

———. 2015. OECD Guidelines on Corporate Governance of State-Owned Enterprises. Paris.

———. 2019. Ownership and Governance of State-Owned Enterprises: A Compendium of National Practices. Paris.

Public-Private Infrastructure Advisory Facility. 2004. Labor Issues in Infrastructure Reform: A Toolkit. World Bank. Washington, DC.

Quality Infrastructure Investment Partnership. 2019. "G20 Principles for Quality Infrastructure Investment." Washington, DC.

World Bank. 2014. Corporate Governance of State-Owned Enterprises: A Toolkit. Washington, DC.

World Bank. 2017. Who Sponsors Infrastructure Projects? Disentangling Public and Private Contributions. Washington, DC.